# A Poem for This Book

"Over the mountain" is a wonderful beginning line to use for writing a poem, a skipping rhyme, or a song.

You could say:
Over the mountain, what did I see?
I saw Brown Bear looking at me!

*or*

Over the mountain, when I was a child,
I found a black cat, savage and wild.

*or*

Over the mountain _____

_____

*or*

Over the mountain _____

_____

*or*

Over the mountain _____

_____

# September Song

"Close the summer" means that you and your friends are back in school. However, you have many summer memories. Create the words, and music if you like, to a song that says "good-bye" to summer.

**Example:**

<u>Backyard baseball all day long,</u>

_____

_____

I remember
In September.

_____

_____

_____

I remember
In September.

_____

_____

_____

I remember
In September.

# An Open and Shut Case!

These things should always be left open:

**Example:**

the cookie jar

_____

_____

_____

These things should always be left closed:

**Example:**

a window in a rain storm

_____

_____

_____

These things may be left open or closed:

_____

_____

_____

_____

# Cries from the Fair

Long ago, when people had things to sell, they would make up a song called a "cry" to shout out so that people would buy their items.

**Example:**

Someone selling flowers could say:
"Who will buy my sweet red roses,
Two blooms for a penny?"

Can you make up a song or a "cry" for these sellers?

Someone selling milk and cheese could say:

_____

_____

Someone selling fruit and vegetables could say:

_____

_____

Someone who sharpens knives could say:

_____

_____

_____

Someone selling pets could say:

_____

_____

_____

# Heigh Ho! It's Off to the Fair!

When I go to a fair or an exhibition...

I love to ride _____

_____

_____

I love to eat _____

_____

_____

I love to see _____

_____

_____

I love to hear _____

_____

_____

I love to play _____

_____

_____

The alphabet is a magic pattern that you can use to create stories and poems.

1. You can write an alphabet story. Start the first sentence with an "A" word and the next sentence with a "B" word. Continue through the alphabet.

   **Example:**

   A   Animals are fun to play with.

   B   Birds fill the air with sounds.

   C   _____

2. You can write an alphabet poem. Begin with an "A" word, then use a "B" word. Continue through the alphabet.

   **Example:**

   A   Andrew

   B   brought

   C   company

   D   downstairs

   E   _____

   F   _____

ABCDEFGHIJKLMNOPQRSTUVWX

Now you can create your own alphabet story or poem.
Will you use alphabet words or alphabet sentences?

_____

_____

_____

_____

_____

_____

_____

_____

_____

_____

_____

_____

**A**lways **B**e **C**ertain
you have fun with the amazing alphabet!!

# Notes I Would Like to Read

Would you like to receive this note?

Hi,

We won't be home until later.
Here is some money so you can buy
supper at the take-out restaurant
for you and your friend.
Write us a note about what
you had to eat, and put it on the fridge.
Have fun!

How would you answer this note?

Write a note that
a camp counsellor might send to a parent.

a dentist might send to a patient.

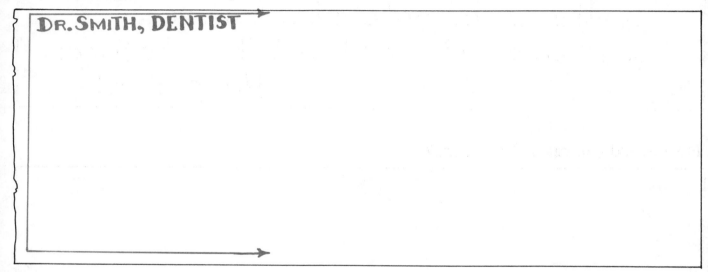

DR. SMITH, DENTIST

an uncle might send to a niece or a nephew.

# A Calendar of Events

Here is a calendar to help you plan your year. Make notes about the things you hope to do each month.

September
_____
_____

October
_____
_____

November
_____
_____

December
_____
_____

January
_____
_____

February
_____
_____

March

_____
_____

April

_____
_____

May

_____
_____

June

_____
_____

July

_____
_____

August

_____
_____

Our number system can be an interesting pattern to use when writing stories and poems.

1. You can begin with "1" and increase the number by one each time you add a line.

**Example:**

I found 1 tiny seahorse in the water at the sea.
I found 2 giant jellyfish in the water at the sea.

I found 3 _____

_____

_____

I'm so lucky
Nothing found me!

2. You can begin with "ONE," and repeat the whole poem each time you add a new line.

**Example:**

Sitting in a tree was ONE black crow.
Sitting in a tree were TWO old buzzards,
                    and ONE black crow.

Sitting in a tree were _____

                    TWO old buzzards,
                    and ONE black crow.

Sitting in a tree were _____

_____

_____

_____

3. You can begin with any number and double or triple it each time you add a new line.

**Example:**

Do you see what I see?

two red ants,

four hairy spiders,

eight _____

sixteen _____

thirty-two _____

sixty-four _____

one hundred and twenty-eight _____

Write a number poem of your own.

_____

_____

_____

_____

_____

_____

_____

# Bubbles and Troubles

I was all set to have my bath on Saturday night.

I turned on the water with just enough hot, just enough cold.

I found my bathtub toys.

I picked out a huge, fluffy towel.

I put in my bubble bath — whoops!

The whole box went in!

First, there were a few bubbles.

Then there were more bubbles.

They filled up the tub!

They filled up the bathroom!

I opened the door and _____

_____

_____

_____

_____

_____

_____

# Fish Thoughts

What are these fish thinking?

# A Fish Story

Use one of your "Fish Thoughts" from the opposite page to write a story.
Who is talking? Where is it happening? When is it happening?
What happened before? What will happen next?

_____

_____

_____

_____

_____

_____

_____

_____

_____

_____

_____

_____

_____

_____

_____

# I Saved the Fish and the Fish Saved Me

There are many folktales about people who captured an animal in a trap
or caught a fish on a hook, and the creature talked to them! They said things like:

"Let me go and I will make you rich!"

"Let me go and I will tell you a secret!"

"Let me go and I will teach you magic!"

Sometimes the people said "Yes," and they were rewarded.
Sometimes the people said "No," and they were tricked.

Write an imaginary story about an adventure you had in the ocean.
You were saved by a fish. One day it came time for you to pay back the fish
for its good deed!

_____

_____

_____

_____

_____

# You Can't Fool Me!

A detective has to examine clues very carefully. Suppose that you discovered the pieces of information shown on this page. Can you put the clues together to figure out what might have happened?

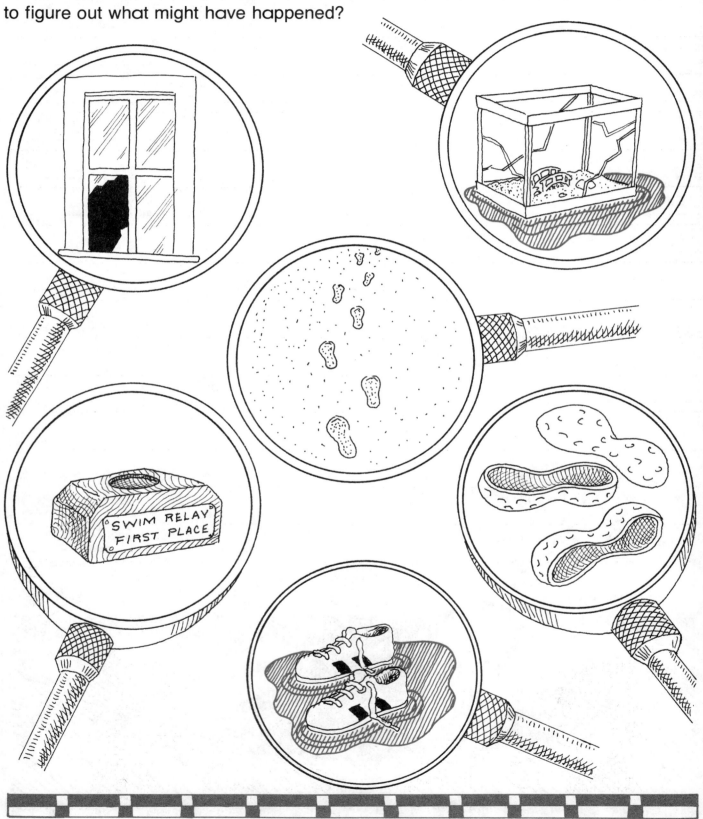

Aha! You solved the mystery!

Detective's Report

_____

_____

_____

_____

_____

_____

_____

_____

_____

_____

_____

_____

_____

_____

_____

# Skipping Along

Dennis Lee wrote a poem called "Rattlesnake Skipping Song."
The first two lines are:

"Mississauga rattlesnakes
Eat brown bread."

Can you write skipping songs or poems about places you know?

**Examples:**

Down in Vancouver,
The whales all swim.

I've been to Halifax,
I've seen the sea.

Find a beginning line, using the name of a place you know,
and start writing!

_____

_____

_____

_____

_____

_____

Write more poems. They could be about other towns or cities or perhaps your favourite places.

Example:
At the lake, at the lake,
I swim all day.

_____

_____

_____

_____

_____

_____

_____

_____

_____

_____

_____

# A Cast of Characters

If you were going to make a movie about a fairy tale, you would need a script with certain characters.

A heroine who will _____

_____

_____

_____

A hero who will _____

_____

_____

_____

A monster who will _____

_____

_____

_____

A woodcutter who will _____

_____

_____

_____

A fairy godmother who will _____

_____

_____

_____

A wicked wizard who will _____

_____

_____

_____

A movie is divided into scenes. Each scene tells part of the story.
Write what happens in one scene of your movie.

_____

_____

_____

_____

_____

_____

_____

_____

# Trading Places

Long ago, people used to trade things they didn't need for other things they needed. For example, a farmer might go to a miller to trade eggs for some flour.

You can create a trading poem.

Found a dollar, found a dollar,
Found a dollar, hear me holler!

I traded the ___dollar___ for a _____

I traded the _____ for a _____

I traded the _____ for a _____

I traded the _____ for a _____

I traded the _____ for a _____

I traded the _____ for a _____

I traded the _____ for a _____

I traded the _____ for a _____

What will I trade now?
I holler, I holler!

# For Sale

Plan a garage sale for next spring. What do you have that you don't need or use anymore? Make a list of things you could sell.

_____     _____

_____     _____

_____     _____

_____     _____

What could you make during the winter to sell at the garage sale? Explain how you are going to make it.

_____

_____

_____

_____

_____

Make a sign to advertise your garage sale.

# Cook a Party!

Giving a party can be fun! However, if you want everyone to have a good time, you have to follow a recipe for making your party a success.

Party Recipe

1. Find a large space where _____

   _____

2. Add _____

3. Shake _____

4. Mix _____

5. Stir _____

6. Pour _____

7. Bake _____

8. Cool _____

That's how to cook a party!

In the story "There's a Party at Mona's Tonight," Potter tries to trick Mona.

Do you think Mona is going to be tricked by Potter's "Aunt Gertrude" disguise?

What do you think she will say to him?

Just in case the disguise doesn't work, create some new ones for Potter to use.

Write what he might say as Mona opens the door.

# A Halloween Stew

Halloween is a wonderful time to write poems. There are so many things you can describe—things you see, things you hear, things you read, things you eat, things you feel, and things you worry about!

Write some Halloween poems for your "poetry stew," using these ideas:

Witch, witch, where do you hide?

_____

_____

_____

Do you hear something? I do! Shhhhh!

_____

_____

_____

The stew I brew: one old shoe,

_____

_____

_____

There are many things to write about at Halloween. Here are some other ideas.

Dear Journal,

If I were a witch
_____

_____

_____

_____

A Witch Goes Shopping

_____

_____

_____

_____

_____

Ghost Tricks

_____

_____

_____

Monster Menu

_____

_____

_____

# Alone in the Woods

Somehow, I got lost!
This is how it happened.

I was _____

_____

_____

_____

I had to survive!

I decided I could eat _____

_____

_____

_____

I built a shelter by _____

_____

_____

_____

Here is a picture of my shelter.

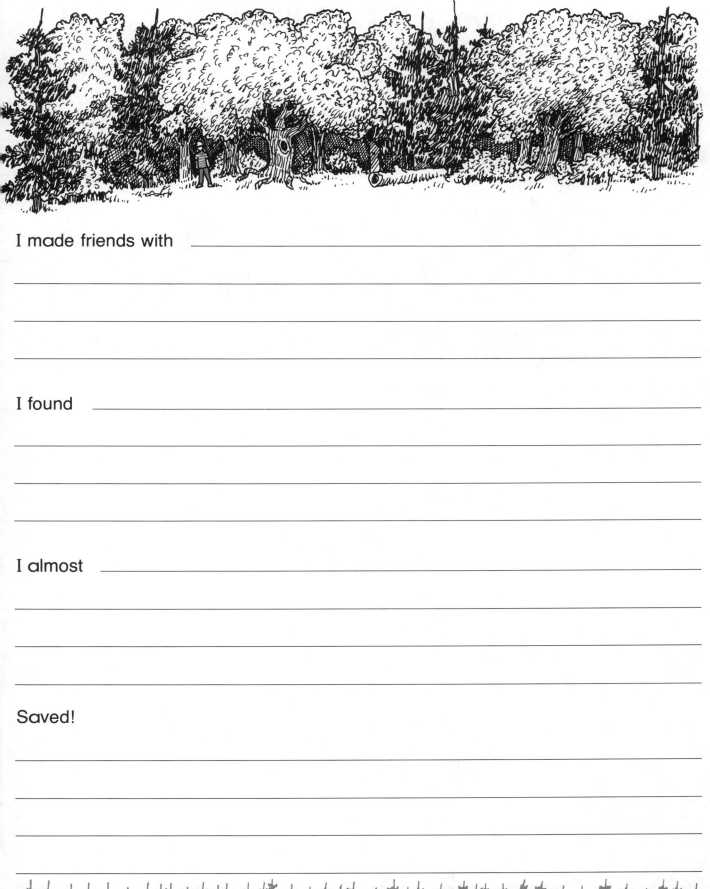

I made friends with _____

_____

_____

_____

I found _____

_____

_____

_____

I almost _____

_____

_____

_____

Saved!

_____

_____

_____

_____

# Dear City Witch

What if Country Witch wrote to City Witch about a country Halloween?
What might she say to coax City Witch to try Halloween in the country?

Dear City Witch,

_____

_____

_____

_____

_____

_____

_____

_____

_____

_____

# Rent-a-Costume

Imagine that you own a store which rents costumes. Make up a catalogue, listing the things you have for rent.

If you want to be
a pirate,
we can help you.

We have _____

_____

_____

_____

_____

If you want to be

a _____,
we can help you.

We have _____

_____

_____

_____

_____

If you want to be

a _____,
we can help you.

We have _____

_____

_____

_____

If you want to be

a _____,
we can help you.

We have _____

_____

_____

_____

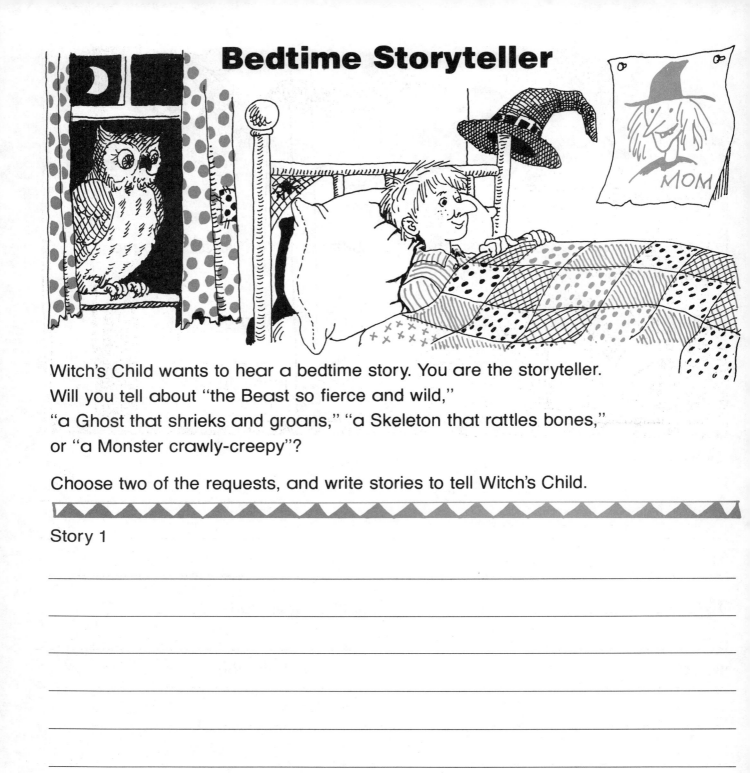

# Bedtime Storyteller

Witch's Child wants to hear a bedtime story. You are the storyteller.
Will you tell about "the Beast so fierce and wild,"
"a Ghost that shrieks and groans," "a Skeleton that rattles bones,"
or "a Monster crawly-creepy"?

Choose two of the requests, and write stories to tell Witch's Child.

Story 1

_____

_____

_____

_____

_____

_____

_____

_____

Story 2

_____

_____

_____

_____

_____

_____

_____

_____

_____

_____

_____

# The Haunted House

Draw a floor plan of a haunted house. Can you tell a story using your pictures? What has happened in this haunted house? When? To whom?

First floor

Second floor

**Basement**

**Attic**

Architect _____

(your name)

# Oh, Yummers, All My Favourites!

In "Yummers," some of Emily Pig's favourite foods are corn on the cob, scones with lots of hot butter and jam, and Girl Scout cookies. What are some of your favourites?

Snacks:

_____

_____

_____

Outdoor games:

_____

_____

_____

Clothes to play in:

_____

_____

_____

Songs to sing:

_____

_____

_____

# My Favourite Story to Tell You

_____

_____

_____

_____

_____

_____

_____

_____

_____

_____

_____

_____

_____

# Someday

Some of Vincenzo's friends in "The Sandwich" had never tried
a mortadella and provolone sandwich. Would you like to try one?
Are there some other things you would like to try?

I have never eaten _____
but someday I would like to try it.

I have never been to _____
but someday I would like to go.

I have never played _____
but someday I would like to.

I have never met _____
but someday I would like to.

I have never made _____
but someday I would like to.

I have never ridden _____
but someday I would like to.

I have never seen _____
but someday I would like to.

# Something New

For someone who is going to eat spaghetti for the first time,
here are some tips:

_____

_____

_____

For someone who is going to ride a bicycle for the first time,
here are some tips:

_____

_____

_____

For someone who is going to _____
here are some tips:

_____

_____

_____

For someone who is going to _____
here are some tips:

_____

_____

_____

# It's So Nice!

In autumn, it's so nice

to play _____

to go to _____

to see _____

to _____

In winter, it's so nice

to play _____

to go to _____

to see _____

to _____

In spring, it's so nice

to play _____

to go to _____

to see _____

to _____

In summer, it's so nice

to play _____

to go to _____

to see _____

to _____

# I Remember...

I remember a perfect day. The season was _____
This is what happened.

_____

_____

_____

_____

_____

_____

_____

_____

_____

_____

_____

_____

_____

_____

_____

What a perfect day!

# Surprise!

Would you be surprised if you found nothing inside your sandwich?
What other things would surprise you?

I would be surprised if

all of a sudden, a bird _____

_____

all of a sudden, all the trees _____

_____

all of a sudden, my teeth _____

_____

all of a sudden, the sun _____

_____

all of a sudden, the school _____

_____

all of a sudden, my voice _____

_____

all of a sudden, everybody's ears _____

_____

all of a sudden, _____

_____

# Imagine That!

Use some of your ideas from the opposite page to write a story.

It started out just like any other day. Then all of a sudden, _____

_____

_____

_____

_____

_____

_____

_____

_____

_____

_____

_____

_____

_____

# Ah Me, What Trouble!

People get into different kinds of trouble. What might be trouble for each of these people?

The worst trouble I ever had was when _____

_____

_____

The worst trouble I ever had was when _____

_____

_____

The worst trouble I ever had was when _____

_____

_____

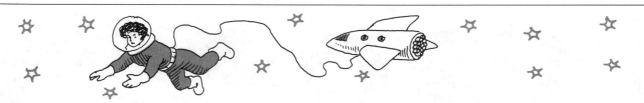

The worst trouble I ever had was when _____

_____

_____

# One of Those Days

It was one of those days when everything went wrong.

In the morning, _____

_____

_____

_____

_____

In the afternoon, _____

_____

_____

_____

_____

In the evening, _____

_____

_____

_____

_____

What a day!

# Street Song Album

Do you play any games that have songs or rhymes that go with them?
Write down some that you know. Perhaps you would like to make up a new one.

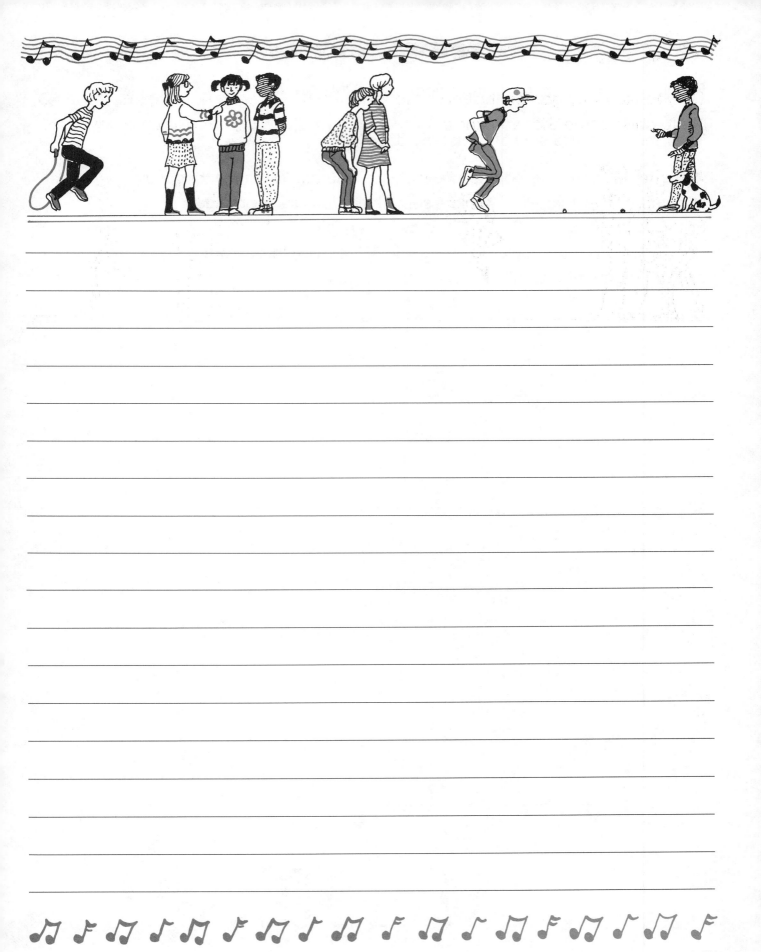

# Quick March!

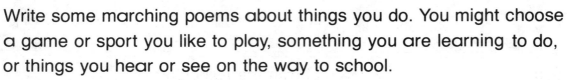

Frank Asch wrote a marching poem called "Apple War."
"One, two, three, four,
They marched like soldiers past my door."

Write some marching poems about things you do. You might choose
a game or sport you like to play, something you are learning to do,
or things you hear or see on the way to school.
In your poems, you could use lines like "One, two, three, four,"
or "Left, right, left, right," or "Five, six, seven, eight."

_____

_____

_____

_____

_____

_____

_____

_____

_____

_____

# On Its Way

In the poem "Food for Thought," the food goes on a journey from the kitchen
to the stomach. Use the same pattern to describe these journeys.
You might want to use words like through, past, over, to, on, or behind.

From my front door,

_____

_____

_____

_____

Look out classroom,
Here I come!

From the raincloud,

_____

_____

_____

_____

Look out puddle,
Here I come!

From the sandbox,

_____

_____

_____

_____

Look out bathtub,
Here I come!

From the field,

_____

_____

_____

_____

Look out stable,
Here I come!

# Come in! Come in!

I eat red things like:

_____

_____

_____

I eat purple things like:

_____

_____

_____

I eat orange things like:

_____

_____

_____

I eat yellow things like:

_____

_____

_____

I eat white things like:

_____

_____

_____

I eat green things like:

_____

_____

_____

# Rainbow Restaurant

Think about all the different-coloured foods you could eat in one meal.
Plan and design a menu for a "Rainbow Restaurant."

Appetizers: _____

_____

Salads: _____

_____

Main courses: _____

_____

_____

Desserts: _____

_____

_____

Beverages: _____

_____

_____

# It's Not Easy!

It's not easy to sleep with crumbs in your bed.
What do you think might make it difficult to do these things?

It's not easy to read a book _____

_____

It's not easy to eat your lunch _____

_____

It's not easy to be quiet _____

_____

It's not easy to stay clean _____

_____

It's not easy to stay awake _____

_____

It's not easy to watch T.V. _____

_____

Add your ideas.

It's not easy to _____

_____

It's not easy to _____

# Oh! Oh!

If you worked in a pop-bottling shop, you would have to be careful not to drop pop bottles. What would you have to be careful about if you had these jobs?

Washing your neighbour's car

_____

_____

Delivering newspapers

_____

_____

Looking after somebody's garden

_____

_____

Making breakfast

_____

_____

Cleaning out someone's garage

_____

_____

# My World to Rearrange!

Have you ever thought that you would like to rearrange your world?
How would you change these places to make them better?

Your classroom

_____

_____

_____

This would be better because _____

_____

Your bedroom

_____

_____

_____

This would be better because _____

_____

Your neighbourhood

_____

_____

_____

This would be better because _____

_____

# You're in Charge!

Suppose you were in charge of the whole school for a day.
Would you make new rules? Would you do different things?
What would the day be like?

_____

_____

_____

_____

_____

_____

_____

_____

_____

_____

_____

_____

_____

_____

# The Sightseeing Sleigh

A ride up Mount Royal by sleigh is still one of the happiest things to do in Montreal during winter. What would you show people if you were driving a sightseeing sleigh around your town or neighbourhood? Draw and write about the special sights.

# Your Hands Draw!

The story "My Feet Roll" is told with pictures. What can you tell about yourself with pictures? Perhaps you can show things you like to do, special places you like to go, or people you like to be with.
Make a picture story about yourself.

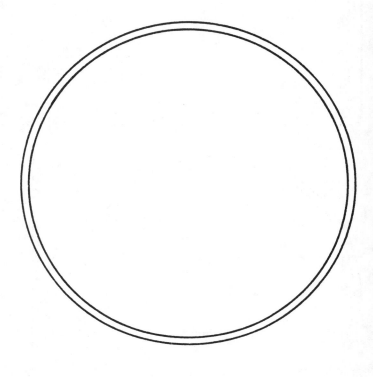
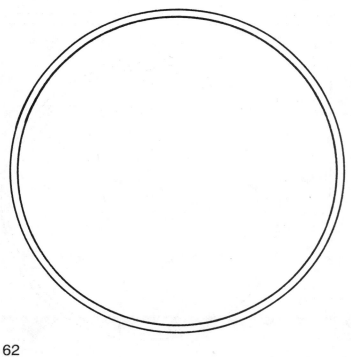

63

# I'll Tell You All About It

In the story "How Six Found Christmas," the little girl had never heard of Christmas. She had no idea what it was.

How would you describe something to someone who has never seen or heard of it? Would you describe its size, shape, and colour? Would you say what you can do with it? Would you talk about how it tastes, smells, sounds, and feels? What other hints could you give?

Explain the following things to a person who has never seen them.

A bicycle

_____

_____

_____

_____

_____

A snowfall

_____

_____

_____

_____

_____

A beaver

_____

_____

_____

_____

_____

A hopscotch game

_____

_____

_____

_____

_____

List three things you would like explained to you.

1. _____

2. _____

3. _____

# Wish a Wish

Jiminy Cricket sings, "When you wish upon a star
Your dreams come true."
Perhaps you can find the rest of the words to this song.

Do you know any other rhymes about wishing?
There is one that begins "Star light, star bright..."

Can you write the rest? _____

_____

_____

Can you think of any stories in which someone wishes for something?
What does Cinderella wish for? _____

What other wishes have you read about in stories?

Story                                      Wish

_____    _____

_____    _____

_____    _____

_____    _____

_____    _____

# I Wish

Write a story about a wish. You can write a story you already know, or make up a new one.

_____

_____

_____

_____

_____

_____

_____

_____

_____

_____

_____

# I've Seen That Before!

Write what each of these signs means.

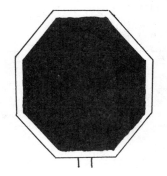

---

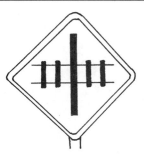

---

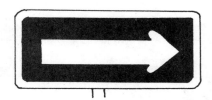

---

---

# Sign Painter

Make a sign...

to sell a bicycle

for a T-shirt

for visitors to your school

to announce a special event

# What I Could Do

If I had a secret on a piece of paper
___ I could hold it in my hand
___ I could keep it in my pocket

If I had a shiny rock

_____

_____

If I had a pair of rainboots

_____

_____

If I had an empty shoebox

_____

_____

If I had a bag of peanuts

_____

_____

If I had a new friend

_____

_____

# What If...

If a friend gave you some dark for daytime, how would you use it?

_____

_____

_____

_____

_____

If a friend gave you some sun for nighttime, how would you use it?

_____

_____

_____

_____

# On the Twelfth Day of Christmas

You probably have heard the song "The Twelve Days of Christmas."
George Mendoza, the author of "A Wart Snake in a Fig Tree,"
used the same pattern to make a new song.

You can do the same thing. Just choose a new theme,
such as a farmyard, kinds of weather, or a candy counter.

On the twelfth day of Christmas
my true love gave to me

twelve _____

eleven _____

ten _____

nine _____

eight _____

seven _____

six _____

five _____

four _____

three _____

two _____

and a _____

# The Useless Store

Imagine that you are going to open a store that sells only useless things.
Make a list of ten things you could sell.

_____     _____

_____     _____

_____     _____

_____     _____

_____     _____

Choose a name for your store. _____

Draw a poster to advertise your store.

Write a radio advertisement for your store.

_____

_____

_____

_____

# Just Saying a Word

In the story "Day and Night : How They Came to Be,"
the fox and the hare each had a magic word to make something happen.
The fox's magic word was "darkness," because he wanted it to be dark
so he could go hunting.

water!

What might each of these animals choose as a magic word? Why?

The elephant's magic word might be "water"

because _____

The beaver's magic word might be _____

because _____

The woodpecker's magic word might be _____

because _____

The salmon's magic word might be _____

because _____

The frog's magic word might be _____

because _____

The porcupine's magic word might be _____

because _____

The mosquito's magic word might be _____

because _____

# Magic Word

What if you could choose a magic word? What would it be? What would it do? When would you use it? Write a story about a time when you used your magic word.

_____

_____

_____

_____

_____

_____

_____

_____

_____

_____

_____

_____

_____

_____

_____

# Home Sweet Home

"The tundra is home for many animals." Seals are at home
on the moving pack ice. Bees, spiders, and beetles are at home
in the small, tough flowers and grasses.

Where would these animals be at home?

Lions are at home _____

_____

Parrots are at home _____

_____

Groundhogs are at home _____

_____

Garter snakes are at home _____

_____

Owls are at home _____

_____

Ants are at home _____

_____

Toads are at home _____

_____

# At Home

Some people live in cities. Some live on farms. Some live on boats. What kind of place would you like to call home? Where would it be? What kind of house would you have? What would be special about it? Write about your ideal home.

_____

_____

_____

_____

_____

_____

_____

_____

_____

_____

_____

_____

_____

# Survival

The caribou's long legs and wide hooves help it pick its way over ice.
The bear's powerful shoulder muscles help it crush seals for food.

Other animals also have special features which help them survive.
What special features does each of these animals have?
How do they use them?

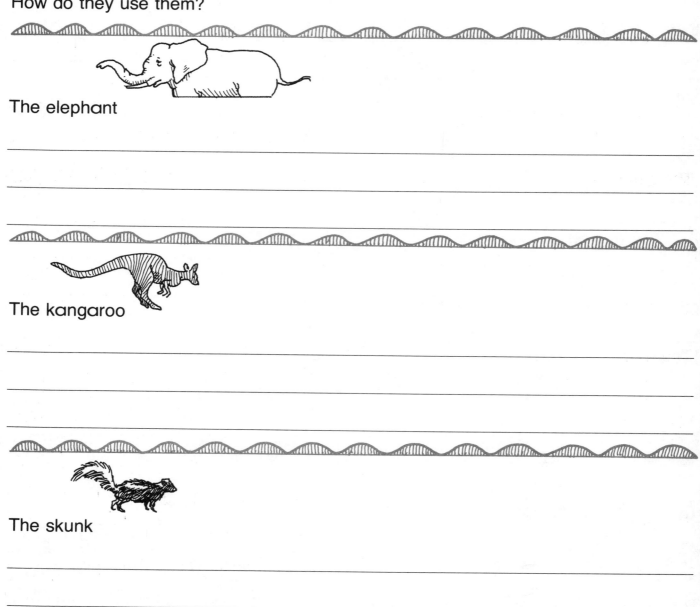

The elephant

_____

_____

The kangaroo

_____

_____

The skunk

_____

_____

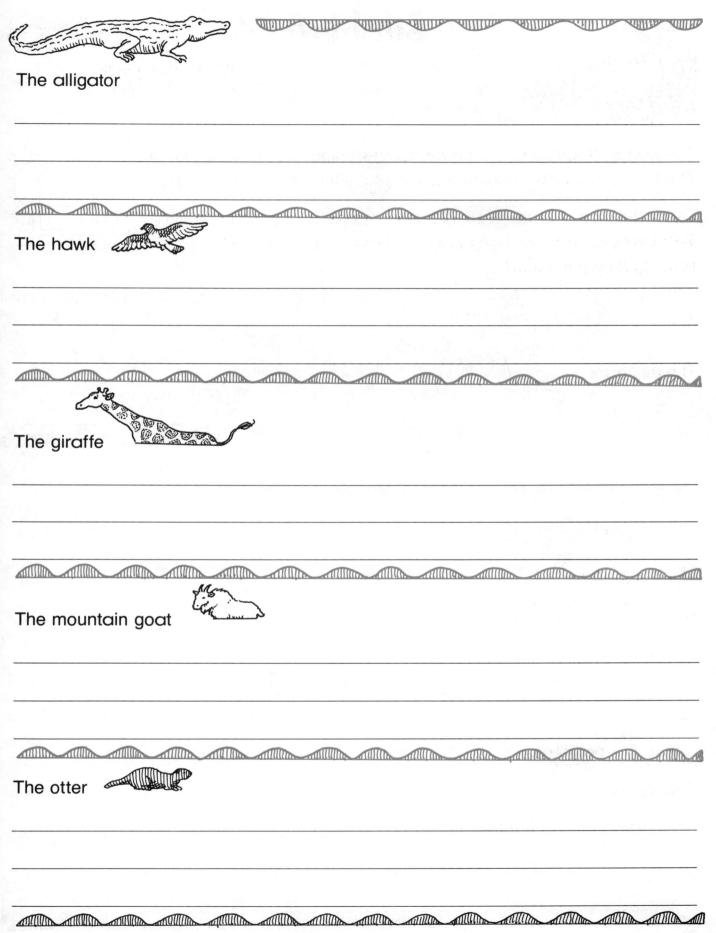

The alligator

The hawk

The giraffe

The mountain goat

The otter

# To Feel Better

Sometimes, things don't work out the way you planned and you get upset.
But there are things you can do to make yourself feel better.
What helps you to cheer up?

When I come home cold and wet after playing in the snow,

this makes me feel better:_____

_____

When this happens: _____

_____

This makes me feel better: _____

_____

When this happens: _____

_____

This makes me feel better: _____

_____

# Things Are Looking Up

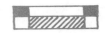

Can you remember a day when you thought everything was going to go wrong, but it turned out O.K.? What were you worried about? What happened to make you feel better? Write about that day.

_____

_____

_____

_____

_____

_____

_____

_____

_____

_____

_____

# Come Along

Imagine that by magic, you can fly, swim, run, and even talk with animals. What will they say? Where will they take you? What will they show you?

Come along,

I will show you where I build my nest and lay my eggs.

_____

_____

_____

Come along with me.

Come along,

_____

_____

_____

Come along with me.

What other animals would you like to travel with? What might they say to you?

Come along,

_____

_____

_____

_____

Come along with me.

Come along,

_____

_____

_____

Come along with me.

# Become One of Them

In the story "The Girl Who Became a Reindeer," Leealaura discovered
the thoughts of many kinds of animals. The animals spoke to her.
She heard about the good and bad things in their lives.

What might these animals be saying?

 # This Is How We Play

In the story "Pitseolak: Pictures Out of My Life," an Inuit woman
tells about the life of her people. One of the things Pitseolak talks about
is the "tennis" game they used to play. She tells how it was played
and what equipment was needed.
Write about some of the games that you play.

A game to play with one friend:

_____

_____

_____

_____

A game to play with lots of friends:

_____

_____

_____

_____

A game to play by yourself:

_____

_____

_____

_____

**These are words you would hear if you played the games I play:**

home free

# Good Advice

In "A Gift For Kuni," Kuni's father gave him some good advice.
He said, "Remember Kuni, you must learn to understand the husky dog before you can build a friendship with him."
What would be good advice for these people?

A new babysitter:

_____

_____

A new neighbour:

_____

_____

A person who is just starting school:

_____

_____

_____

Think about a time when you were given some good advice.
What was the problem? Who gave you the advice? What was the advice?
Did you take the advice? Write a story about the advice and what happened.

_____

_____

_____

_____

_____

_____

_____

_____

_____

_____

_____

_____

_____

# As Regular as Winter

In "Children of the Yukon," the ravens returned to town "as regular as winter." Write about other things that happen "as regular as winter."

Every year:

_____

_____

_____

Every month:

_____

_____

_____

Every week:

_____

_____

_____

Every day:

_____

_____

_____

Every minute:

_____

_____

_____

# Oh, I Wish...

These things happen all the time. I wish they didn't.

_____

_____

_____

_____

_____

These things don't happen often. I wish they did.

_____

_____

_____

_____

Even if it could only happen once in my lifetime,

I wish _____

_____

_____

_____

# Listen...What's Going On?

In the Yukon, "the sound of dogs barking and children laughing often means a snowshoe race is taking place."
Even if you can't see what is going on, you can sometimes guess from what you hear.

Here is a "sound picture." What might be going on?

The sound of bells ringing, doors opening, children running,

often means that _____

Create some "sound pictures" of your own.

The sound of _____

often means that _____

The sound of _____

often means that _____

The sound of _____

often means that _____

The sound of _____

often means that _____

Choose one of the "sound pictures" from the opposite page.
Illustrate your "sound picture." Show what is happening,
where it is, and what or who is making the sounds.

Write a story about what your picture shows.

_____

_____

_____

_____

_____

_____

_____

# If Only...

Have you ever thought about what it would be like to be another kind of creature? What would you see? What would you hear? What would you smell? What would you eat? Where would you live? What would you do?

If I could be a whale in the sea, _____

_____

_____

_____

If I could be a bird in the sky, _____

_____

_____

_____

If I could be a squirrel in the forest, _____

_____

_____

_____

If I could be a polar bear in the Arctic, _____

_____

_____

_____

If I could be a snake in the desert, _____

_____

_____

_____

If I could be a butterfly in the garden, _____

_____

_____

_____

It would be fun,
but I like to be me!  ME!
Here's why.

I _____

_____

_____

_____

_____

# Looking Back

Think of all the stories and poems you read in *Over the Mountain*. Use this page to write about some of the things you remember.

Something that made me laugh:

_____

_____

_____

Something that I would like to read to my family:

_____

_____

_____

Some characters I would like to meet:

_____

_____

_____

Some of my other thoughts about the book:

_____

_____

_____